Dear Barbara,
It was such a delight to
meet you on the roof with
Pat — and to find that we
have much shared resonance
about our rich Catholic roots.

After God

Enjoy the
theological
ride!

Michael Whelan

Tinteán Féin Press
Dublin

And a tip: I suggest
you read the poems
in sequence. They
unfold like a novel

After God

Published by Tinteán Féin Press. All rights reserved.

Some of these poems have appeared in slightly different versions in The Coachella Review, The Eloquent Atheist, The Leitrim Guardian and the Martin Stannard August 2013 Collection.

Special thanks to mentor poets Dermot Healy and Terence Winch. Thanks also to Joyce and John Cooke, St. John's Abbey–Collegeville, Minn., Carol F. Brown, Constance Walker, Darcie Kortan, and Margaret Osburn.

Cover photo by John Cooke,

Library of Congress Cataloging-in-Publication Data has been applied for.

ISBN-13: 9780692341452

DEDICATION

To the late Dermot Healy
Ballyconnell, Sligo

Dazzling poet, amazing mentor, marvel of a friend

He was one of the lions of contemporary Irish writing.
We met in Ellen's, a "last pub before Boston," on the
windswept wilds of the West Coast of Ireland. He
mentored generously and insightfully
in my making of this collection.

Contents

Before After God

I was born in Saint Claire's hospital on 56th Street in Manhattan, the first son of a young Irish father born in County Leitrim and an Irish mother born in County Roscommon. He was the son of a farmer, she the daughter of a coach maker. They had met and married in New York. In the Irish way, we were taught to call them Dada and Mama.

Dada entered the grocery business when he arrived in America. By the time I was growing, he owned his own grocery business. With his entrepreneurial Irish charm he made it into a small epicenter in our Manhattan neighborhood of Morningside Heights.

When I was eight, he sent me, my brother Gerald and my sister Sheila sailing off with our mother for a whole and wholly marvelous summer in Ireland.

When I was 18, I joined the De La Salle Christian Brothers, the religious order whose brothers taught me in our Irish-Catholic New York grade school and in high school.

Twelve years later, at the end of the 60s, I left the Brothers, Church, faith and God. And entered *After God.*

These poems flow as a story — like a novel.
To experience their narrative dimension, the poet suggests
they be read sequentially, first to last.

In the kitchen of my brain

The atheist agnostic mystic
fundamentalist free-thinker Cabalist
Episcopalian fire-eyed heretic Muslim
Buddhist Jewish ritual-incensed Catholic

holds dialogues and trialogues
and multilogues all night
inside himself inside
the kitchen of my brain.

Chain smokes his arguments,
slams fist on the table,
squashes cockroaches of
all opposing views

and most of all of
gullible believers. All
night he keeps me up, opening
and slamming my refrigerator door,

popping cans of god beer inside
my being, running with his
fingertips riffs of god, no-god, god
irrelevant, new god, god

erased like the Nixon tapes. I wish
to hell he'd go to hell.
But if he makes to go, I beg
him stay but please

don't let the neighbors
know he's here
because I fear downstairs
the cynic sophisticate

agnostic and
his smart-ass buddy atheist
will think I think I have
a soul.

I. FIRST KNOWING

THE JUNK MAN AND THE SISTER

1.
At four my little body,
little soul, join like
play pals. Alone we rock

and rock and
rock hours
on the old arm chair.

Joy to the world!
The Lord has come!
I sing it in body.

I sing it in soul.
I howl in protest
when finally Mama

brings in the junk man
to take away the chair
I've worn down to

trash. In theatric futility,
in tears I pull
against the junk man and

stomp my feet.

2.
In first grade
God, stolen by the junk man,
comes around each day, ethereal

feminine, hooded and cloaked
in black, hypnotically close
over me in Sister, checking

the little block letters I practice
in my copybook. When she draws
near, the air around her

carries the scent
of her veil — like God breathing
over my head.

Big black Rosary beads hang
from her waist beside my ear. I listen

into their rattle — secret strange
clicky sounds from God.

GOD'S PAPER EYES

Sister Steven Helen
smiles

and lifts the cover page
of the huge pad on the tripod

to reveal

to my five-year-old, wide eyes:
GOD

in bright
comic book pastels.

Against a paper sky of blue, I see
an old man, white-haired,

long white beard. He wears
white sheets.

He sits on a gold chair
that's on a cloud.

This is:
God, the Father, who

made you to
know, love and

serve Him.
There is anger in his eyes.

Around him people with wings
and gold hair bow down.

These are:
Angels,

*who live in the sky with God
in a place called Heaven.*

I look for the green of trees
and grass. None.

With her wooden pointer
Sister taps God's paper eyes.

*God is watching
you*

*all day, all
night, all day, all night*

*to see
if you are good,*

*but especially to see
if you are*

bad.

THE SACRED HEART

Sister tells us God has
a son. He is a man. But he is also God.

His name is Jesus. She turns the page
in the flip pad and there he is.

He looks nicer than that God the Father
who's been watching me from the cloud.

Jesus is young. He has long brown hair and he looks
you in the eye from right here, not from up there.

Everyone seems to like him better than God.
Mama likes him specially. She keeps a picture of him

in a frame
on the wall in the hall.

Under it she has a shelf with a little candle.
She lights it every day. In the picture Jesus points

to his chest. He's had an operation. You can see
into his heart. A flame is burning out of it.

Mama shows me there are thorns on it. I see
drops of Jesus's blood dripping from where they cut into it.

She tells me this is *The Sacred Heart*. It burns
with love for us and suffers thorns for us.

I get used to seeing Jesus with a flame.
Sometimes Mama lets me light the candle under him.

Sister tells us that later this year we will
make our First Communion. I don't know

what that is yet, but she says in it
we will receive Jesus on our tongue.

I wonder how he will fit on my tongue.
And if he will burn it.

CAUGHT BREATH

1.
I am all in white — white short-pants suit,
starched white shirt, little white tie,
white shoes and socks —

and magic in its scent, a fleshy white
gardenia pinned winsome
by Mama to my white lapel.

At the marble altar rail I take my turn
to kneel. In gold embroidered stole
the priest draws near.

Corpus Domini nostri Jesu Christi
he whispers in strange words over me
custodiat animam tuam…

Oh Lord I am not worthy
sings the choir — so tender, sweet as candy —
that Thou should'st come to me.

Then from his golden cup
he lifts a round white circle
and lays it like paper on my tongue.

2.
All of a sudden I feel God
become
inside me

dropped
down from his cloud,
shape shifted

as Jesus
nested now
in me.

3.
Ever
so gentle on my tongue
I carry Jesus

to my place
in the pews. Not so,
my first-grade classmates.

They've swallowed their hosts.
They jostle on the kneelers. Turn
heads round. Nudge

each other, itching
for First Communion parties
soon to come.

4.
Odd child, I do not
move. I am lost in
my wonder. I am

caught breath.

LADY GREGORY AND MR. YEATS

1.
Mrs. Bailey has put a fresh lump
of sugar in her cup of tea. Across the kitchen table
Mama sits and listens, sipping her own.

Mrs. Bailey is real old. Her hair is white.
Tied up in a bun. Her dress is black and frilly.
"And Lady Gregory said to Mr. Yeats . . ."

Mrs. Bailey loves to talk about those two people.
"And when we went to Paris, Lady Gregory always
called for. . . And I said to Mr. Yeats, I did . . . "

I don't understand what Lady Gregory called for
or what she said to Mr. Yeats. But I like the two
of them.

Like aunt and uncle ghosts,
they appear in our kitchen whenever
Mrs. Bailey comes.

2.
Later in life I will understand that years before
she came into our life to help
at our modest apartment on Lexington Avenue,

this old lady had been nursemaid
in the household of Lady Gregory.
Surely then our Mrs. Bailey walked the lanes

of Coole Park. And saw
the very swans the Poet glided
across his page.

So also might she
have gotten to listen in — perhaps
from a hallway — to hear

the Poet speak
for the first time:

I will arise and go now.

UNDER THE CARROTS & APRICOTS

1.
Under the carrots and apricots —
under the onions and oranges —
under the elegant price signs
hand-lettered by Dada

and stapled to wooden sticks planted in the produce —
under the striped green and yellow awning
that filters sunlight so mellow
through the cracks of the fruit and veggie crates —

under these unders, we hide out.
Our cap guns are loaded. No one knows
we're down here under the world of grownups.
We are Roy Rogers, the Lone Ranger, Tonto.

We scout outlaws and Indians. Their horses are
the passing legs we spy on the street, the legs of Mrs. Messman or
Mrs. Shaughnessy and the other ladies who come not just to shop
but to banter with my handsome Dada in his Irish charm.

2.
Later we steal out of our hideaway. Watching us
as we emerge is a filigree of stone eyes of elongated
saints and daemons. They are carved in stone
above the giant iron doors of our neighborhood colossus:

the Cathedral of St. John the Divine.
As if in medieval Europe, Dada's grocery sits
straight across the avenue at its foot. "The second
largest church in the world," claim the tour-bus guides.
Cleverly, Dada has befriended the guides. So they steer

their tourists into our store. All manner
of visitors come under our awning from strange
lands — including America (a foreign country to
our New York kids' heads) — for a cool drink on a hot day.

They enter bearing costly cameras.
The price of our Pepsi
silently inflates
from a nickel to a dime.

3.
Another make believe is Louie's, down the street.
He fixes busted radios. We love to gape
into his wizard's cave of dark and dust, crazy with
wires, electric tubes, exposed guts of radios.

Last week we lucked on a totally amazing sight!
A white glow flickered in the dark on a flat glass
no bigger than a book. The flicker: our Lone Ranger and Tonto—
riding horses, chasing outlaws!

We'd heard of TV—but never seen one.
We climbed over each other to gawk.
Louie usually shooed us off but he was nice that day.
He let us in.

But I got so excited,
I knocked over a radio.

Louie whacked me.
Word shot up the street
to Dada in the store. Down came

Dada, his apron still on—
a meat cleaver
in his hand!

He'd left the cash register
open behind him!
The whole neighborhood
followed him.

Never you
ever
dare hit
my son!!

I was shaking. Didn't know
what
to think, what
to feel.

Louie apologized and apologized.
In the end, they shook hands.
Then Louie took me and my pals
to Doc's soda fountain in the drugstore.

He bought us sundaes — gleaming
with whipped cream,
a cherry on the top.

But the guys topped that
when they said,
"Your dad!

— Wow!"

THEY STAND TO REASON

The old peasant lady told Mr. Yeats
she did not believe in hell or ghosts, but
as to the Fairies: "They stand to reason."

When I was eight we sailed to Ireland
for a summer. I took with me

a small square of red cellophane
that tinted the world surreal rose

when I held it to my eye.
It was my secret way to see.

I carried it, companion in my pocket,
up the gangplank when we left New York.

I peeked though my cellophane all that summer
at the fields and castles and clouds of Ireland

and thought I saw, alone and on my own,
a secret world. Though perhaps I was not alone,

but rather child taken
by spirits the Irish call the fairies

to see for a season through the mystic eye
of my Celtic ancestors.

At summer's end I touched that tiny cellophane
window in my pocket when I came

down the gangplank in New York.
I felt its amazement at crossing the sea twice,

seeing so much hiding wonder,
and coming home.

Later in life, I understood:
children see the touchable world

full of spirits, full of fairies.
Most grow up and leave their early wonder

in abandoned toy boxes.
I never can.

A BULB LIGHTS UP INSIDE HER

1.
The block is buzzing. Boys squirting water guns, flipping
baseball cards, spinning yo-yos. Kid noise everywhere. It's 8:30
a.m.

A whistle blows. Silence. We know the routine. Little Catholic
soldiers,
we form ranks by grade. There on the top of the steps to Ascension
School

stands Brother Augustine, our black-robed principal, a whistle in his
mouth.
No talking allowed. Second whistle. Walk in line up to our
classroom.

Keep in line. Talk on the way and you get
a penance: "Write 100 times *I must not talk on line.*"

Our class follows Brother Gabriel. We'll be with him
all day, all year. Each morning, we size him up.

Is he smiling? Good. Some fun, maybe even laughs, with him
today.
Is he sour? Watch out! He hits. And you get *I-must-nots* for the
littlest thing.

Either way, he's a giant. Knows everything — mental arithmetic,
history, perfect penmanship, geography, the catechism, music.

Once a week he takes out a Victrola and gets us lost in
the *Pilgrim's Chorus.* Tells us it's from an opera called *Tannhaüser.*

He's a Yankee fan. When the World Series comes around,
he comes into class with a radio! We listen with him to the play by
play — like we're hearing God.

Sometimes he talks to us like we're grown-ups—he fumes
against McCarthy, his communist hearings on TV. We nod our
heads like adults.

2.
Every morning, the principal comes to visit. I look forward to it.
He's so smooth, this Brother Augustine. He never hits.

He always calls us "gentlemen." And he always has
a new gizmo to sell.

Today it's a plastic statue of our Blessed Virgin.
A bulb lights up inside her.

*See? And if you screw off
the bottom, you will find, gentlemen — look:*

*this pair of rosary beads. A fine gift for a boy
to give his mom on Mother's Day.*

50 cents. Neat! Mama will love it.
I decide on the spot to save up to buy one.

3.
Today when I leave class, Brother Gabriel calls me aside.
Mike, you're a quiet kid. I bet

you think a lot about God, right.
How did he know?

He tells me the brothers have noticed me. *Have you
ever thought that someday you might*

*have a call from God —
a vocation?*

A bulb
lights up inside me. I glow,

part awe, part fright.
My nostrils puff with pride.

Would you like to join a bus trip for
a day in Barrytown?

It's in the country — where you go to become a brother.
I have pictured me there.

I ask Mama if I can go. She talks to Dada.
He calls me aside. *Yes, I'm sure Barrytown is*

a nice place, and we all admire the brothers. But you —
you're still too young to think about that life.

Boys should live at home. Right? I nod.
I'm afraid to disagree. Embarrassed, I lay Barrytown aside.

But the seed is planted. A strange ground in me
has been waiting for the likes of it.

A GENESIS OF YES

1.
You can spot us on the dining balcony: four boys,
imaginative, bookish, a bit weird,
no good at sports.

We are *Gems Incorporated*. Purported producers
of a gem a day of literature — a sinuous single
line — composed collegially over coffee and lemon meringue –

that with nickels we release from the glass-door dispensers
at the Horn & Hardart automat on 72nd Street.
We have taken to calling this balcony our *board room*,

chosen for its pretense of class in marble and brass —
and yes too, because it's cheap, and just a block
from the De La Salle Institute, where we go to school.

Listen as we remark on our school building,
which we at Gems are prone to
reference aesthetically:

classic brownstone, gilded cage elevator
(alas, for faculty only), fireplaces in every classroom,
library of slanted glass roof, a virtual atelier!

Observe the street population round our school:
Jeweled old Jewish ladies,
trailing shopping carts, share the sidewalks

with skinny, strange young men,
eye shadowed and rouged,
in slick pomaded hair, wrists fluttering,

promenade queen-like on air.
"Different, honey," liberal Mable Goldstein calls them —
"gay" not yet in the language for them.

Listen in next to the neighborhood:
Floating on the early autumn air
over the backyard alley gardens

come the scales of opera singers
entering the open window of our Latin class,
counterpointing our drills of *amo-amas-amat*.

Go inside our classrooms: The zeitgeist
of the neighborhood seeps into the teaching.
This is a school where

your favorite English teacher is called
Brother *Aelred*. I love the name sound. He's silver haired,
his mellow voice refinely modulated as the scales of our opera
singers.

He introduces us to the texts of Broadway dramas
playing live just three subway stops away.
He attunes me to savor — to my surprise —

elegance in 18th century American prose
in the letters of the Founding Fathers.
I picture myself as a Brother Aelred.

2.
If I were where he is
I'd be in a world more serene
than in the quirky world we have at home.

Mama is a dreamer-worrier, prone to be
overwhelmed by life, sleeping till noon, so
home is a mess

of clutter I daily try to clear.
The Christian Brothers, I imagine, live in no
clutter. I want their ordered life.

Dada in mid-life crisis suddenly decides to sell
his grocery business. Mama protests. There are
fights in the night. I want to escape the fights.

The Christian Brothers make a vow of poverty —
holding nothing as their own. If I were one, I could, unlike
my father and my mother, live free of money fights and worries.

My adolescent head makes these lists.
They are whys — or rationalizings —
for the strange choice of life I weigh.

3.
But deeper than rationalizing whys,
I feel a strange, alluring
irrational why.

A why
in the memory
of a scent.

Like a doe in the woods
I sniffed it first in the gardenia
my mother pinned to my lapel

on my First Communion day.
I smelled it again drifting
round the veils of the nuns.

I even detected it enigmatic
in the air near the brothers,
hovering in their robes.

It returned rich and insistent
in aromas in the parish church:
in its perfume of burning beeswax candles,

in its heady smoky clouds of incense rising,
in its overwhelming fragrances from endless Easter lilies
flooding our Holy Thursday altar,

and closest to me, in my own
altar-boy cassock and surplus.
Each scented instance

opened in me
an intuition
of a presence — sacred yet immanent.

Each instance beckoned me out of me
as if a marker laid for me by
the Divine.

That scent was
the ultimate
genesis

of the *Yes*

I spoke
inside me
in my senior year.

THE NEWS

I break the news
to Mama and Dada.

It means leaving home. Taking
the brothers' habit. Making vows.

Hesitantly they grant
their *Yes*.

"But," prods Mama
"wouldn't you

rather be
            a priest?"

I LOOKED DOWN, NOT INTO THEIR EYES

"Can I offer you a high ball, Brother Brian?" asked Mama. She had readied the Seagram's and 7Up—the Irish Catholic drink of choice. Sometimes she sent me embarrassed to school with a carton of Camels for the brothers. She said the brothers are human. They must like to smoke.

"Well I won't say no
to your gracious offer,"
chuckled Brother, debonair
in black suit and white clerical collar.
He wore
gold cuff links.

Mama had seated him to notice our encyclopedia in the living room bookcase. All the furniture was newly polished for his visit. Dada wore suit and tie. This was a big night. A visit from clergy—even from brothers, who were not priests—was a prized honor for a Catholic home. For tonight's visit, the brothers sent Brother Brian, one of their most socially adept men—skilled in the art of reassuring uneasy parents about to lose their sons to the Christian Brothers.

We looked nervous.
Brother Brian countered
with charm—a pause, and a smile
at our framed image
of the Sacred Heart in the hall.

"I see you have
a good Catholic home here,
Mr. and Mrs. Whelan,
...and a fine son too!"

Years later, when I finished my training and became a teaching brother, Brother Brian and I would be in the same high school faculty. I would learn then that despite his self-assured and polished way, the drink was an addiction. He would disappear for days in his room. But tonight he was impeccably at his peak and after small sips and niceties, he launched the sales call.

"Michael's first year, Mr. and Mrs. Whelan, will be in our novitiate in Barrytown. It will be a year of:

intense prayer and
spiritual formation.
You might call it

God's boot camp."
Brother smiled, sipping
his highball judiciously.

Mama chuckled
politely as if
she was in the know.
Dada did not smile.

Brother Brian continued. "Then Michael will move on to four years at Catholic University in Washington to get his B.A., and after that he will come out of formation and become a full-fledged teaching brother—like yours truly!"

"And how often
will Michael come
home, Brother?" asked Mama.
I knew the answer. They would
not like it.

"Often, once he is
a teaching brother. But the order
does not allow
visits home during formation. You can
visit Michael twice a year."

Silence.

"But that's five
years, Brother!" said Dada.
I didn't expect my father
to attack Brother.

Then Dada looked
directly into my eyes.

"Do you
      really want to
           do this, Michael?"
                  My mother joined the question with her
                  eyes.

I felt like a traitor on trial.
I looked down,
not into their eyes.

"Yes. I want to be a Christian Brother. I feel I
have a vocation."
I was sure.
I was unsure.

"It's hard," said Dada. "We raise
our children all these years
in the Church,
and then!…They are

gone like this. Is this
what God does?
What do we get for all
our sacrifices, Brother?"

Brother Brian answered.

"The gift of a son's
vocation, Mr. Whelan, surely
a high honor
to you from God."

Silence.

"Well, if it's what
you want, Michael . . ." said Dada softening.

"And it *is* a gift from God,
a high honor," said Mama, trying

not to cry.

LAST SUPPER

It is the night before
I leave home.
I am thrilled.
No one else is.

They are thinking
this will be
our last supper
at the dinner table.

In this kitchen, our unofficial
sacred space, we would gather
late at night as if called. Dada just in
from closing the store. One by one

we would come — to have perhaps
a glass of milk,
a slice of cake,
a cup of tea.

But in fact we came for the magic.
The clock over the stove stopped.
We became easy
as around a hearth.

Dada would dial the radio to
Big Joe's Happiness Exchange,
a show where people phoned in
weird catastrophes.

As a family, we had a taste
for the odd. It was our private pantomime. But tonight
Mama, Dada, big sister Sheila, little brother Gerald
are silent.

We start to eat.
Dada takes a bite.
Suddenly he is
weeping.

I've never seen
my father cry.
He runs from the table.
Dashes into my bedroom.

I don't know what to do. Mama surprises me.
"Go in," she says, "Talk to
your father." I am stunned. She has opened
a door I thought could never open.

I feel a birth begin in me
from boy to man –
her trusting me to open my own
heart as my own, on my own.

I rise from the table. Frightened,
but with that heart, I walk to
my father, carrying
all the distance between us.

To this father who
loved me in indirect gestures —
but never said so
one to one.

I may never be as brave again
as in the moment
I opened my bedroom door
to talk to my father for the first time.

He was sitting on the edge of my bed.
So sad, so lost.
So like the lost boy
I thought I was to him.

"I hope we gave you a good home here,
Michael," he said weeping.
His words erupt in me
a second birth this night.

We weep together. I know the cost
to him to break his binding. The same fear,
he knows, has
bound me.

After that,
he always greeted me
with a kiss, till he died
at 93.

BEHIND THE WALL

THE RIDE. Brother Aelred waited down on the street in the car the Brothers sent for me. Mama would not come down. She said she couldn't bear the neighbors gawking. So in tears at our door, she kissed me. I rode the elevator down alone with my stuffed suitcase. It was lonely. But I was smiling. It was my ride into my life. And I knew it.

BARRYTOWN. Ninety miles up the Taconic Parkway, we turn into a long curved driveway sweeping above a steep ravine. The novitiate stands in the distance like a lost castle. For a year, 50 of us arriving today will be sealed off from the world. No news, TV, radio, phone. No word of what's on the hit parade. They call it *cloistered.* I'm taken by the exotic in the word. I like its mystery.

THE BELL. A heavy ancient hand bell. We will take turns as bell ringer. The bell will call us every hour. To prayer. To meals. To prayer. To manual labor. To prayer. To study. To prayer. To sleep. It seems to expand time — its toll governed by the *horarium,* the Latin for our ancient, inflexible, near-sacred novitiate schedule.

MEALS. We eat monastic style — in silence. One of us reads aloud from a book, usually pious. Some are nutty pious, though they're not supposed to be nutty. We love those best. We stifle laughs but common sense wins out.

HAND SIGNALS. At table, we are finally getting the hand signals right. We look like deaf mutes. We don't talk. To say please pass the coffee pot, we flash an index finger from a fist. For sugar, an index finger and a pinkie. Wise guys deliberately let slip a lone middle finger.

MARTYRS. I loved the tale read aloud today at breakfast. A martyr stands up and plunks his head back on after it's chopped off. Breaking silence, some guy whispers, "Pardon me, but that's my head," out of earshot up at the high table, where the Novice Master and the two brothers on the faculty preside like Puritan elders over our meals.

SNOOPING. The Novice Master laid out our first mail today in the common room. Each envelope had been slit open and read. I think it's wrong that they do that, but that's the rules. Maria Mooney, who has a crush on me, has sent me a letter on flowery paper scented with perfume. The Novice Master says tell her to stop.

DECODING MAMA. Mama's first letter came today. O-my-god, I forgot! Only my sister Sheila can decode Mama's handwriting. Holy Ghost, help me. I imagine a response from Him. "Read it not word by word but for the gist!" I do. Miracle! Her meaning emerges from the blur. Dada's first letter came too. He says I am now "in God's pocket."

THE HABIT. I was measured for mine today: the Christian Brother's robe—long, black, sleek, straight, with its ancient white French *rabat* hanging from the neck in two flat flaps of plastic. Originally they were linen. They look like the tablets of the Ten Commandments. I felt suddenly holy when I tried the robe on for my fitting.

"A-B-C." It's heady to change your identity at 18. We will each take a new name as a brother. The one we choose must begin with an A, B or C. That letter code distinguishes New York brother names from brother names in other provinces of the order. There are 20,000 Christian Brothers around the world.

AELRED. The A-B-C rule lands a lot of weird names among us: Albeus, Alphonsus, Benignus, Barnabas, Calixtus, Cagetin—all saints. Mine is announced as "Brother Aelred Terrence, known in the world as Michael Whelan." My choice of Aelred is to honor Brother Aelred, my English teacher and model, but even more because I think the sound *Aelred* is neat.

A WILL? Today we wrote a will. It was weird. We are all kids with no property and we don't expect to die soon. The Church is big on reminding us we will die. It's kind of spooky. Very Vatican.

HABIT TAKING. After our two months of "postulancy," I was accepted today, with 50 other guys, into the order as a novice. We entered the chapel wearing our robes for the first time, the *Te Deum* blasting jubilantly from the organ, flash-bulb cubes on our visitors' cameras popping all around. Our families, aunts, uncles, friends all came. Mama cried.

SILENCE. It's in the Rule. In the novitiate we are supposed to "keep silence" outside recreation time. Nobody really does. I tried for awhile, then gave up. The ones who stick with it are called *up the wall*—super pious types who take it all too seriously.

LATIN. My four years of high school Latin make our prayers in Latin almost interesting. Other guys who didn't take Latin complain they're gibberish. We recite the Psalms in Latin. We chant at Mass in Latin. We say grace before meals in Latin.

LAUGHTER. The Brother Provincial, the head man, visited us new novices today. He told us that novices are notorious for happiness. You know, he's right. In spite of our straightjacket life, we laugh constantly. For sanity, I guess. But oddly, also for pure joy.

SHOTS. Once a week—it's in the Rule—we do a ceremony where each guy asks the group to "have the charity to advertise me of my defects." We think it's nuts. We call it shots. Some guys refuse to shoot. Others shoot for the fun of it. I get shot for "making a sloppy genuflection." Little do they know I have an ingrown toe nail.

GABE. Brother Albinus Gabriel. He's new as a Novice Master. Has new ideas. "Please, brothers, not those tacky plastic icicles!" he says with pained face at Christmas. All year long he will try to rid us of tacky taste. He secretly smokes. It's not allowed. I was shocked when Calixtus told me. He says everyone knows. I'm out of it sometimes.

ALBIE. Brother Albinus teaches us. He has wide spooky eyes but he jokes. And he tells us all about the newspapers we don't get to see. Yesterday in his class he gave us mimeo copies of a *New Yorker* story on the "Beat Generation." He says that's our generation. The heady whiff of mimeo ink on his yellow pages got everyone sniffing them like we were the Beats.

CHANT. I'm lost in plain chant. Even the blocks of notes up and down on the Liber page enchant me. Music locked in mystery. And the sound that comes out of us when we chant together! We take on a single mystery voice. It's hard to believe that's us guys echoing through the hollows of the stone chapel like voices from another century.

GRIPERS. None of all this is a surprise. Each of us visited for a weekend here last year, to see novitiate life firsthand. But now into November, most guys start to gripe. They can't wait till the year is over. Not me. The God who caught my eye as a little boy is here.

FLO. The jocks call him "Flo" Foley. He has a constant five o'clock shadow but fingernails long as a hooker's. I wonder the superiors don't ship him home. During recreation he cries tears as he plays sad love songs on the piano. He tells me in a whisper, "I can get out of here in 24 hours."

FLUKING. Today, a cold mean February day, Gabe announced in his typically pained voice that one more of our group has "left the order." Ten have left so far. This we call *fluking*. This time it's Laverdi. His exit was handled under cover of dark, out of novices' sight. The news hits me each time like a death. Some guys sneak up to Laverdi's locker to see if he left behind his contraband Aqua Velva.

LAVERDI. Until he fluked, he was the most colorful guy here. Arrived in suede loafers. Created his own in-house industry of gold-sprayed driftwood from the Hudson, which he transformed into glitzy centerpieces. Disobeyed every rule. Fought a shouting match in the dormitory with Charlie B, who insists on having the windows open in the freezing cold. "Fuck you, Brother!" he yelled in the dark at Charlie, breaking the *grand silence,* that is the rule from sunset to sunrise.

ICE SKATING. Winter has hit. It's pure snow and beauty outside. Yesterday Gabe gave us a surprise: a few free hours to ice skate on the cove at river's edge by the railroad. It was totally frozen. We opened our coats like sails to take us over the ice. It was all trance — we flew on beat-up skates we got from what was called "common stock" under the coat racks in the basement.

SPRING. The seasons here hypnotize. The liturgical year we follow matches them and gives them stunning depth. So May is like a Disney spring. Buds blooming everywhere. This morning we went in procession chanting around the grounds to bless the crops. It's called *rogation.* "Totally pagan fertility rites," says Albie.

FUNERALS. Oliver Joe died today. He's an old French brother who ran the garden. We have been reading about the ancient mystics. To me he was a living one. Mystery-filled eyes, as if looking constantly at the face of God. We will bury him in our cemetery, the bell tolling as we follow his coffin along the road. We could as well be in the 17th-century France of our founder Saint La Salle. We have buried five of the *Ancients* this year. That's what the old ones are called.

THIRD KNOCK

First Knock
is winter shattering sleep
with icy clang of hand bell

that calls us to rise silent
and move mute in black robes

down dormitory stairs into
a dark of stone-walled cloister passage

its lone radiator
hopelessly hissing

under frozen windows
through which first sight of dawn

is stars over distant Catskills, moon
over Hudson's slow black flow.

Next oaken doors
open into candle flicker

arching against white chapel walls,
as entering we sweep our fingers

over the chill sponge of holy water,
cross ourselves and genuflect

to greet Jesus, veiled presence
on the altar in his tabernacle.

Second Knock
is of novice master's
knuckle on wooden pew

echoing off the stone walls
to cue us groggy-eyed

young men — boys fresh
from New York City boroughs —

to open each our red-gilded
Imitation of Christ

and ponder in it the medieval
broodings of Thomas-a-Kempis:

The more I go out into the world,
The less I return a man.

Third Knock
comes when novice master's knuckle
raps again

signaling command to close all books
and freeing us, young

monks, to meditative wander
in peaked woolen parkas

alone over winter grounds
where in the awe of dawn

my novice soul wakes at last
to speak speechless

inside the new wonder
I am coming to know as God

while along the distant pines at river's edge
the New York Central rushes past,

its long and longing whistle my prayer
in the ice-holy air.

MOTHER NATURE DISPOSES

1.
The year of novitiate that our gripers felt would never end has ended. Kneeling at the chapel altar with a lighted candle in hand, we proclaim our first vows: poverty, chastity, obedience. They make us officially Christian Brothers.

Next stop, back to the world. Or rather, out of the novitiate and on to De La Salle College, our collegiate house of studies in Washington, D.C. There we join some hundred upperclassmen. We will all study as undergraduates at nearby Catholic University.

But we are still semi-cloistered. No *leaving the property* except to go to CU—and only in our own blue shuttle buses, driven by our classmates. First day of fall classes we step off our bus in our robes and onto the CU campus.

It's flooded with seminarians, nuns and other orders of brothers, all in robes too. But it's not all otherworld. The real world will sit beside us in class in the other half of the student body: partying non-holy college kids—of both sexes.

2.
But *Strictly no
socializing
with the secular students*!

So rules Brother Leo Kirby, our dominating new director.
How else could Kirby curb our libidos and hold
the old college party instinct at bay?

OK. God proposes—but Mother Nature
disposes. She feeds us
sex hormones like chicken soup.

What can we do? We pour them into
Olympic-intensity study. Learning becomes our games.
Our De La Salle College becomes an Acropolis of scholarship.

On the CU campus, they call us Christian Brothers
the *curve raisers*. We usurp the *A*'s that
smart, partying lay students hoped to glide into.

But study burns up only so much
sex drive. There's overflow.
And with the opposite sex off the table

and out of reach, a same sex
option teases. It's Mother Nature again.
To cut her off at the pass, Kirby watches

like a castrated hawk. He rants
against *particular friendships*—a classic monastic
taboo. He cites word-for-word the holy dictum

of our French founder, Saint La Salle: *No brother
shall be seen too frequently in the company of
another brother.*

Like the rule of silence, it's honored
in its breach. For most, the friendships are
Platonic. The few who venture farther, if caught,
get shipped.

But it's the early '60s. In less than a decade,
belief in vowed sexual abstinence will
crack apart like a dropped vase.

Out of the order will go
most of us, eager to
catch up, find women, make love, marry.

Or for the 10 percent whom
God and Mother Nature
made gay—like me—

find men.

DUCK ON A BROOMSTICK

Dr. Giovanni Giovanini. Urbane, continental,
bony and short, with signature head of wavy white
hair. Nickname: *Duck on a Broomstick*.

They say Giovanini for years visited
Ezra Pound, politically incarcerated as insane
nearby in St. Elizabeth's, the DC mental hospital.

Today in Giovanini's Senior Symposium
I deliver, as English major,
my senior paper — on Hopkins's *Windhover*.

The poem — wild, inventive, mystical, thunder-spiked —
dances and flips. My paper not quite. Yet Giovanini
does not — like other arch-eyed professors — attack.

Instead, he opens
a line of questions —
each teasing

out of me new perceptions to flip
my thinking and dance me inside the word ecstasy
of that daylight's dauphin dapple-dawn-drawn Falcon.

Then Giovanini releases me

on a bow bend of understanding
riding the wings of two masteries at once —
the poet's and the teacher's.

Later as teacher brother,
I will not forget,
old *Duck on a Broomstick*,

how you taught me how
to stir a student heart
in hiding.

II. UNKNOWING

CANADIAN CLUB & JOHNNIE WALKER

1.
Lyndon Johnson, as Vice President, speaks at our CU Graduation.
I land a gold Phi Beta Kappa key. I give it to my beaming mother.
Our five years of semi-cloister are over. Time to get back into

the world. My first assignment: St. Joe's, Buffalo,
one of our best schools. I arrive educated but with life still to learn.
I learn soon that here "out in community" the monasticism

goes way down. We will pray only morning and early evening.
And the first evening we skip prayer for this:
Gathering in the lounge at 5:30. The typed notice is

posted by the boss, Brother Johnny Broils.
Gathering for what? At 5:30 I find out.
Into the lounge comes Broils carrying bottles

of Johnnie Walker and Canadian Club, unlocked
from the closet in his room. This is *wockles.* At it
the older monks, who have the system down, pour

their whisky four fingers high — to ensure they get
a good jolt before the bottles are locked up again.
From these pros I will learn to drink at the varsity level.

Here God fades from center stage.
The focus is on running a school — a very good one.
Our alumni — avidly loyal — go back generations.

Football is king. When we play our Jesuit rival,
it's front page in the city papers. I land the role of overseeing
the marching band. I can't even play a kazoo.

On TV, Ed Sullivan brings on the Beatles. "They'll never last," I say.
In November, Kennedy is shot. We cancel the sock-hop.
Soon the Viet Nam war is drafting men my age. But as clergy

I get a 4D draft deferment — somewhere near the paraplegics.
The times, they are a-changing, sings Dylan. The Church is too.
Out of nowhere the new Pope John calls a Vatican Council.

2.
Everything Catholic set in stone begins to move.
Nuns appear on the front page of *The Buffalo Evening News*
in their new short skirts and short veils. Nuns show hair!

Guitars at Mass irk the older monks. Our rule changes too.
Instead of the robe, we get the choice to dress in suit and tie,
and to take back our birth name. I do, on both counts.

I announce to the boys I'm now *Brother Michael Whelan* — no more
Brother Aelred. Regardless, behind my back the kids still call me
Flash — untutored adolescent irony — because I'm still spacey.

In June, the end of the school year, new posting edicts
come from headquarters — and a list of monks
who are *defecting* from the order. This always comes

like a blow to the gut. These are guys, many of them friends, you
expected to live your whole life with in the order. June
after June, the length of the list grows and grows.

SECOND COMING

1.
Each night on Broadway,
the dancers in *Hair* chant
The Dawning of the Age of Aquarius
in the nude.

Uptown at Manhattan College
the spirit of Aquarius is
dawning theologically.
I'm here on a year's sabbatical.

With me are 40 or so nuns,
priests, brothers — none in
the nude, but most no longer
in religious garb.

2.
The theology here is probing,
imaginative, unabashedly
upending the Vatican's dogmatic
apple carts. We do

new-style Mass, altar-free
in the college lounge.
Create our own liturgies.
For Eucharist, no papery

thin white host. Instead, a hefty
loaf of bakery bread
we break by hand and pass
from hand to hand as Jesus did.

We become full-time theology bookworms.
In no time, it's a ritual
round midnight to pile into cars
and ride down the Riverdale hills

to the all-night diner
under the el. There
among burgers, beer, cigarettes
and Neil Diamond on the juke box,

we talk into the night —
theology, life, theology,
politics, theology,
love.

3.
Three nuns — Janet, Grace, and Eve — each
of whom will, before the year is ended,
leave their orders — fall in love with me. But I'm gay.
Don't know how to tell them nor deal with love of women.

Lots of tears on both sides.

Giles, a brother from New Orleans, comes
into my room. "I'm smitten!" he cries. A very sexy
woman called Belinda flirtatiously caught
his eye as they passed the Eucharist

from hand to hand. After mass he learns she
is Sister Belinda. A chaotic romance
ensues. In a year, I'm at their wedding party.
"A marriage made in heaven," says Belinda with a wink.

4.
In Biblical exegesis we
deconstruct the sacred texts.
The *Gospel Truth*
turns out to be elusive,

self-contradictory in places,
mythically embellished in others.
The four-gospel canon was chosen
politically — ignoring the Gnostic gospels,

whose wild poetic mystic
take on Jesus was deemed heretical by
early Church authorities determined
to have all march to one flat doctrinal drum.

And then there's Jesus as God-man —
a divinity he never claimed in Mathew,
Mark, or Luke. It was the newcomer
Paul who packaged him so.

The virgin birth? The star
of Bethlehem? The visit of the Magi?
The death and resurrection
of the God-man?

None original.
Similar motifs circulated
in neighboring
pagan religions.

5.
The more of cloudy
dogmatic bath water
I spin out, the more
I start to ask:

Should
this baby
survive its bath?

DAMASCENE MOMENT

And priests in black gowns were making their rounds,
and binding with briars, our loves and desires.
                William Blake, The Garden of Love

1.
Sorry, says the Pope:
No condom. No pill. No
matter what.

Scratch the sorry. He has
no apology. His is classic papal
proclamation: case closed.

In a dead tongue, like
a dead message,
he issues it in Latin.

Humanae Vitae (Of Human Life),
his new papal encyclical. It hits me
in the face, front page, *New York Times*.

This is the straw — not unexpected — to
break the failing camel's back
of my Catholic obeisance. No

matter that these new Pope taboos
have not to do
with me, a brother making no babies.

No, it's his flawed and
soulless syllogisms
of celibate logic blind to love

and to the starving infants
this edict will generate dispassionately
from the poorest of the believing poor.

With the clarity
of a Saul of Tarsus,
knocked from his horse,

my blindness lifts to see: This
papal-strangled church
can no more be my church.

2.
A tectonic creedal shift
moves under me.
Cracks spring up and down

my orthodox belief structure.
The deepest fissure is in the notion
of *dogma* as a way to know.

I have been reading the Tao:
Those who say
don't know.

Those who know
don't say.

ATONEMENT

Angry Father Demands Blood
of Only Son — "Jeezus!" we mutter
at the tabloid details
over our coffee and toast.

Why the shock?
Isn't this the blood thirst
sanctioned — glorified —
in our crucifix?

That icon of the mad trade
between man and his savage
Bible god — a brutal transaction muffled
by the word *atonement*.

We learned to trace its sign –
forehead to waist,
shoulder to shoulder,
down on our knees –

in adoration of
      Our Father
pleased by
      atonement

— instead of crying
Shame!
Shame on You,
God!

STEALING GOD'S EYES

*"But of the tree of the knowledge of good and evil, you shall not eat of it,
for in the day that you eat thereof you shall surely die."* Genesis 2:17

Why in God's name forbid
the fruit of the knowledge
of good
and evil?

What sin in knowledge?
Wrong question.
Ask instead: What
knowing

would a jealous
Biblical God
not
want known?

Maybe this:
the one bit
of which one bite
could dethrone Him.

As in: What if
Good-and-Evil were
the binary code
for the whole of creation?

To break the code you must
pull it from the tree of life —
eat
of it, like Eve.

Bite into it
deep,
deeper,
deeper.

But to broach
this brazen deed
you must have
doubt.

Great science
starts
from doubt.
Think Copernicus.

Q.E.D.:
The forbidden fruit
may have been
Primal Doubt.

When a man
—in this case, woman—
doubts boldly,
she sees

as if divine.

She steals God's eyes.
And so, pulls down
the house on her race.

Precisely the vengeance
a jealous Bible God would smite
on one who steals his eyes.

No wonder then
she'd have to
leave the garden.

And, of course,
could never be
a priest.

DIVORCE CAN BE NASTY

Curmudgeon!
Despot
Lightning hurler
Crank upstairs

Over
Lauded

Over
Feared

Elusive as a cockroach
When the light switch flips

Biblical Wizard of Oz
That's You

We're through!

TWO CALLS

Are You watching—
whispering wordless
Leave?

The same You who
called me
in?

The You again who
calls me
out?

Or are the calls
only me

hunting
me

hunting
You?

EXIT PRAYER

God, grant me a bomb
to blow up
your throne.

God, grace me the acid
to burn off
your face.

God, gift me the tongs
to pull out
your eyes.

God, hand me the ax
to chop off
your head.

And God:

      When I wipe you out of here,
don't pop up over there.

      When at last I un-gender you,
don't morph back into that Old Man.

      When I close down heaven and its clouds,
stop floating on them in the top of my head.

For the love of God,
      God, help me
kill you.

For the love of God,
      God, get out of
my light.

A TIME FOR BURNING

1.
Each day bit by bit
its dry needles
dropped to the floor,

till the time came
when the dead tree's deadness
became undeniable.

This despite the dazzle
of lights and trinkets
with which we dressed

those green needles
the day we brought it home
fresh cut with the scent of life.

The parents deemed it now
a fire hazard.
It had to come down.

Wistfully we
dismantled
the trimmings.

2.
It is like that too
when I finally
take down my Catholicism.

It is I, not the parents,
who deems this dead tree
a hazard.

And so I unstring the maze of dogmas
with which the Church directed me
to girdle my God.

From the top of the tree comes down
Maker of the Universe,
Aquinas's *Uncaused Cause*.

Next I pull off the ponderous
Augustinian glass ball
of *Original Sin*

and its match, *Divine Judgment*,
flashing God-gone-mad
in *Dies Irae*.

Lower down the tree I pluck
from the dried and brittle branches
the stringed lights of

Revelation
and the anthropomorphic *Lord God*,
their bulbs gone out

tangled in church tinsel
of dogma and knots of
Infallibility.

After them, shattering as they hit
the floor, fall the garish glass figurines
of *Atonement* and *Redemption*.

On the top of the pile
I dump the
Will of God.

LEAVING

This plain
June day, hazy and hot,
alone I plunk into the back
of Dada's station wagon,

borrowed for the day,
a few boxes—books, photos,
papers, clothes—the little I carry
after 12 years as brother.

The last to be packed
is an afterthought:
the black robe on the back
of my door. Surprising myself

I fold it
with an ache
into the bottom
of my last box to go.

In it I fold away
Brothers,
Church,
Faith.

Let them rest, I think,
in the bottom box
of my soul. Tattered
from the soul's first season.

III. UNKNOWING SQUARED

WITH A CAPITAL "F"!

I land first
like a lucky roll in Monopoly, on the top floor
of the Helmsley building—a Manhattan icon.
Under its archways down on the street

streams of taxis zig like yellow metered bugs
from Park Avenue North to Park Avenue South.
I've landed my first job at this pinnacle. I'm a novice
dirt-digger reporter trolling for *not-for-attribution*

insider scoops for *The Gallagher Presidents' Report.*
It's read—even when not admitted—by every
corporate CEO in the know in New York.
Go for the jugular, Mikey. Fuck 'em! –

with a capital F! shouts the slight but legendary
Barney Gallagher, impeccably dressed
in custom-tailored suit. He thrusts his arm
dismissively toward his 33rd floor office window.

I follow his eye out of it, straight up Park Avenue
to the high-rise corporate dens of our prime
chief executive prey. Barney is training me
how to interview those big-time guys.

I'm over my head but I love it. I had never read
The Wall Street Journal till Barney hired me.
Now I read it everyday like it's *People* magazine.
Barney is old-time Irish Catholic, a self-made

millionaire. He tells me in his street-smart New Yorkeze
he likes to hire ex-priests and ex-brothers like me.
They work harder, Mikey,
on their second bounce.

Obligingly I shift my eye
from God
to the jugular
of the CEO.

BEYOND OPINION

I no longer go to mass. No longer pray.
Nor want to. I no longer hear

the gushing of my old wave of God
mourning and wailing on alien shores.

I imbibe instead a nectar
of martinis after work

in Sardi's and the Algonquin.
I sip and savor the secular

like an epicure,
human again.

If asked of God I answer *agnostic*.
Beyond opinion. Through with belief.

I eschew even the atheists.
Atheism is a belief.

I am in the place my soul
needs to go.

I stay a long while.

It's a good place
to methadone a deity addiction.

I WONDER DID YOU KNOW

I watch the priest anoint
you, Mama,
with the oils of the dying.

It is a year now since I stopped
believing.
I have not told you.

He has lighted candles
beside you and placed
in your view a crucifix.

It is a year now since I stopped
believing.
I have not told you.

He marks small
crosses of holy oil
on your forehead and hands.

As the oils touch, your breathing
goes serene. A glow, a peace,
takes over your frail face.

I have not told you.

As a boy in catechism class,
I always thought it spooky,
this *Sacrament of the Dying*.

Till today I have never seen
the ritual. Till today, death
has never come this near.

After the priest leaves
we take turns beside you, holding
your hand, sharing it with your Rosary.

I have not told you.

I say your Hail Marys
aloud for you. You look at
me eye to eye.

I have not told you.

Later, Dada calls us suddenly to come.
You have opened your eyes so wide.
I've never before seen ecstasy.

You breathe in.
You go still.
There is no out breath.

I wonder
did
you know?

I LIKE TO VISIT EMPTY CHURCHES

I like to visit empty churches
I like especially empty Catholic churches
I like the intensity shaded in their shadows

I like
the quiet
the half light
the dogma stilled
the crackle of votive lights
the residue of incense in the air
the lone candle burning glass-red in the sanctuary lamp
the way the sounds of the street come in to pray, meekly muffled
the thrust and soar of nave and transept opening spaces of sacred in
stone

I like the way the emptiness remembers —
When our parish church was wonder's epicenter
When to enter it, girls pinned hankies on their heads as makeshift
hats
When altar boys in sneakers sent clouds of incense rising from
golden censers
When High Mass hypnotized us with Latin chant and organ peal
and thunder
When Eucharistic processions of the golden monstrance under
swaying canopies dazzled our faith-full eyes

I miss all those whens of before they went
I miss being a Catholic
But I am beyond return

Yet I hold the memories
To light like candles in
The emptied sanctuary of my soul

DE LA SALLE VESPERS

1.
Vespers mellow, the sun
that late autumn afternoon seemed to know
what we were about.

And as if for us had stretched up North Capitol
and dropped down through the avenue
of pines we used to walk in robes.

US Government Property blustered
the sign at the foot of the driveway. All
who enter here must *WEAR A SEAT BELT.*

Point well taken — when you are about,
after four decades, to collide
with an icon of your past.

In its Tudor facade, the building waited lonesome
at the top of the hill. Empty of all
but the days when it was our De La Salle College.

Around it, six-foot-high, a chain-link fence.
But the afternoon sun, a seasoned
Vespers sun, was too wise for fences.

Easily it slipped through the links.
And coaxed us follow. One among us
found a hole in the links.

And one by one as in procession
we squeezed through — felons trespassing
on our past.

2.
Inside we picked our way through broken
glass and broken cinderblock.
New owners were remaking the building.

Walls that were lay smashed, markers
for memory, gone. But out of the rubble
memory winked.

Soon we could pinpoint,
finger certain,
each place, each space.

Here I slept standing up in chapel
through my meditation. Odd monk.
In this stairwell, arguing one-to-one
over explications of Eliot, we butted brains.

And here most special of all:
the common room, our study! For this space,
it was as if the sun knew.

Through broken windows it streamed
harvest rich, low and long across the floor.
The rubble turned to gold.

And we became again who we were
in those young dazzle days when learning blazed
among us like a star at birth.

3.
We left with two keepsakes.

The first a vision — sighted in the shadows,
the etching of *Christ the Teacher* weak now as a whisper
across the brick of what was once the chapel wall.

The second, spotted in a pile of rubbish,
fragments from the old chapel windows –
stained glass of green and blue and gold.

Through these the sun of long ago
moved over us, young monks at prayer
or nodding off at prayer.

We pocketed
each
a fragment.

STRUCK MATCH

In dawn on my porch floor by the sea
I spot among the books I've brought for summer, one
I threw by ironic chance into my bags:

Seeds of Contemplation –
Thomas Merton. A well worn paperback
from my days in the Brothers.

Price then: 75 cents —
when I still believed in "contemplation."
Why not open it? For old times' sake.

I do. Maybe it's the feel in the hand
of an old book once loved. Or that old
signature prescience of Spirit in Merton's writing.

Whatever it is, I draw back into
the who I was — the wondering who, whom I've lived without
so long now.

The way dry wood holds fire
ready to leap out at the touch of a struck match, a fire
muffled in my dryness has met its struck match.

Of a sudden
I flame.
I am burning
mad-rich in awe at the simple elemental wonder of
HERE.

There are no words.
I see nothing,
hear nothing.
I am not imagining.
A sense beyond sense urges

LET GO.

I do. And when I do
the old wild wonder wakes and rips
in ripples through my limbs.

This wonder I've known before–
in miniature

in my solitary
odd-boy First Communion's
caught breath

in the lone awe of novice dawn
hearing an ice-holy longing
in the New York Central whistle

in the markers laid
in my memories
of a scent.

VICE VERSA VICE

1.
All I did that dawn
was look within—
after a long

long time
of not looking
within.

And out of a no
where inside within:

Shazzam!

those old firecrackers, bolting
wonder head to toe!

What was
that?

A *What*?
Or a *Who*?

Pure dumb matter—
brain cells

with a kink
in their DNA?

Or brain cells
captured

by bright pure
Spirit?

2.
Hello, old friend—
You Who or What.

You've danced in me
again.

But if you're a What,
your dumb cover

has been outed by
Mr. Einstein in his special

relativity, revealing
matter and energy

as in essence each
the other.

Might you, pure dumb matter,
be

the flip side
of pure bright Abyss?

And vice versa?
Yes. Vice versa vice. All the way.

A MYSTERIOUS BRILLIANCE

*"He to whom this emotion
is a stranger, who can no longer pause
to wonder and stand rapt in awe,
is as good as dead; his eyes are closed."*
                                        Albert Einstein

1.
"A mysterious brilliance" — that's
what he said he found
when he delved as no man before him
into the mysteries of time and space.
He'd even speak of its "dear Lord" —
But of a "personal God?"
No. He always answered *No.*

It's as if Mr. Einstein had two heads.
His physicist head saw *no Person.*
His poet head played with a *dear Lord.*
What's a body to do?
Move unapologetically between the two,
that's what he'd do.

Mr. Emerson believed, but not in the Word.
Instead of *God* he proposed *Oversoul.*
But then came the question:
Is *Oversoul* a person? "It's not,"
he answered, "that *person* is too
big a word for God
but that it is too small."

2.
I invite Mr. Emerson and Mr. Einstein
to tea in the garden in my head where
I grow my own unreason.

There I listen to them joust about
the possibility-impossibility of

a YOU in every you
       a WHO in every what

a YOU without a face
       – its absent face

its enigma,
       its enticement –

that Ultimate behind the mask
       we call the universe:

      YOU ^{2}

HOLE IN THE SOUL

Some days I believe in You. Some not.
But even when not, I still wonder about You.
The space You fill before I unbelieve You
never leaves with You.

I once had a cat for a month. Drove me crazy
with allergies and pooping on my washing machine and
never coming to me when I called. Just like You.
I gave the cat away. Came home and found

it left its space behind. Empty. Sad space. I missed that cat.
But only for a while. Soon the cat's empty space was gone.
Like any emptied self-respecting space, it had cursed me,
shook the dust of me from its feet, and left to follow the cat.

But not Your space. It always stays
when I empty it of You.
Hangs a vacancy sign in its window. And
through it, stares blank back at me.

OK then. Come home.
Just for tonight.
Tomorrow I will unbelieve you again.
But tonight come

fill
the hole
in
my soul.

KEEP THE FAITH

1.
"Keep the Faith." The parents of Ireland wept the words—
that ancient goodbye to emigrating sons and daughters.
Best wish. Best prayer. Their heritage. *The Faith.*

As boy-man of 17 my father boarded a ship to America.
Along with his bag, he carried
the Faith.

He brought it to New York.
And kept it all his life. I still remember him
by his bed each night, kneeling to pray.

And so the Faith came to me to keep.
For a time, I kept it.
Then I did not keep it.

2.
 Tonight, like a pressed flower I folded away
decades ago in the book of who I was

the Faith falls out on the floor.
I have opened the book. Or more accurately,

the book has opened itself. I pick up the dried
pressed faded Faith. And discover in it a wonder—

that signature transcendent wonder my ancestors lived as
immanent in Ireland's earth and sky and sea and life.

Wasn't that the same wonder I felt tug me as child
fascinated by *God*, whoever He was—if He was?

The same wonder who never left me
when I thought I left it?

The same wonder who leapt of a sudden
through my body that dawn on a porch by the sea?

3.
*"Oh, Lord, I believe. Help
my unbelief."*

No, Lord. Belief is not a test
to pass to please a God.
Belief is like a door

in the soul. You need never
go near it. But If you do,
it opens to a space

called *Faith*, a graced
space the soul keeps
for falling into wonder.

And unbelief? Doubt?
Another graced space. To contest
me. To shock me

at the madness in a *Yes*
that would steal
my soul
off into the wilds of wonder.

Doubt — to wag its finger
warning wonder,
if opened
full, can devour the self

out, out,
out of itself.

Doubt — faithful
keeper
of lost Faith.

PASSAGE

There was only your labored
breathing

and the Cavan fiddler
playing faintly from the CD

and you, gone transcendent,
closed eyes filled with light.

Across the icy Hudson dark
below the window by your bed,

under cover of barges ferrying cargo
downriver to the docks of New York

I spied the ancient lantern:
Charon's boat come on word

of dead to ferry for a coin
over the treacherous waters

of the Styx. But you
would need no Charon. You —

your spirit winning as all else
in you failed — had by now negotiated

your own Styx treacherous even with
confusion

and words — your dazzle with them —
lost to your tongue.

And so tonight, out of your failing body,
like a ship's light in the dark,

glowed the child-man who seventy-seven
years ago sailed your Irish dreams

into the harbor
of New York.

But there was here tonight
no longer

harbor of mind nor body
to hold among us

the Who you had
become.

So I kissed you —
as you did me each time

you greeted me since that night
we broke our boundaries.

And as the child honored
to see you into your glory passage

I silently
bid you:

Go.

THE WORD

From the start it was
an upstart of a word.

It pointed frightfully beyond itself.
Then kidnapped the hearer

out of all words.
To protect themselves,

authorities who heard it
tried immediately to cage it

and dry with definitions
the wildness out of it.

But they could cage only
the letters in it.

The wildness of its meaning
never left, never spoke a word.

It's where that word
sends you is its meaning

as is where that word
comes from,

and it keeps on, keeps on
pointing.

CAN WE TALK?

Will we ever talk again, the way we used to
in the old days of chapel visits in
that dark silence when I told You my cares
and heard You comfort me, counsel me?

Those words of comfort counsel: They were mine.
But who's to say You did not inhabit them.
That's the trouble with being a human trying
to converse with the divine. There's no telling

who is talking. You — or just some
popes or ayatollahs or faith-based
politicians — like George Bush, who said
you personally OK'd his war.

So what's a soul to do
who tries
to talk to You?

Let go
the must
of hearing words

and let soul and
all fool questions
ricochet

intimately
within the silence
of a You.

Still, I'd love to talk again
like way back
when

You
were my
Imaginary Friend.

Or was it I
who was
                  Yours?

PLACEHOLDER

For Erica Van Acker, September 11, 2001

I.
God is a placeholder word.
Even if we think

there be none
we need One.

A place to hold all our
no-words. A place

outside-inside space —
to hold our unholdable:

the Enigma, the Wonder
in here.

Whether there
be One or be none

is beside the point — because we
are the point: each a cheek

kissed
by the Enigma.

II.
God knows, Placeholder,
You've teased

me all these years
I've looked for You

up maybe in ideas
or inside out

across universes
or under-inside quarks, me never recognizing until
tonight, sore with memory,

You kissed me once
goodbye.

III.
The kiss came—ten years gone now—
in that goodnight from her lips

she left in
a light on my cheek

outside her Eastside door
the last time she

touched me: that week before
the Second Tower

fell on her
forever.

IV.
So singular a kiss—prescient
as if we both unknowing sensed

what was to come. That night
she placed it mysterious

on my cheek. And it glowed
as if I'd never known

a kiss before—

all my way
across 63rd Street

all my way
down Second Avenue.

Her Placeholder.
My Unholdable.

Never filled since then
when I walked away

without her,
down the street

where she lived.

.

CLAY FEET

Yesterday, when I was walking exiled
in clay feet in the cool of the evening
outside the garden of the Tree

of the Knowledge of Good and Evil,
God slipped into a pair
of clay feet too

We walked foot to foot for some time
and being that close, I noticed that
God is:

More earth than air
            More of here than of there
                        and all of now

Bounding in and out of ifs
            Abiding boundless
                        inside is

Transcendent most
            when curled
                        in the crannies of creation

As much a She as He
            and She is also we
                        and God forgive me, also me

Creeds cannot catch Him
            nor churches cage Her –
                        He keeps no throne in Rome

She has no test for us to pass
            no will for us to bow to—
                        He burns no hell

She yawns when She hears "O God" intoned
       by preachers over the pews
              but He cups His ear when

a lone soul whispers
       "O God, help me make it
              through the night"

That's when He may lean in and that's when
       the lone soul may be opened to
              to a silence

That may come like a hum
       out of the ground
              of Nothing

As in
       Nothing to do but be, dear,
              Nowhere to be but here

THIS IS WHERE WE CAME IN

Of God I am
of three minds:

      There is One
      There is None
      None and One are One

Of the three
I believe
each best

Then I back
away to come at the question
round another tri-corner:

      The question emerges like a primal echo
      The question bears no answer
      The question suffers no answer

To which, in theatric futility,
in tears a little boy pulls
against the junk man and

      stomps
      his
      feet

When all is said and done, how do we not know but that our own unreason may be better than another's truth? For it has been warmed on our hearths and in our soul, and is ready for the wild bees of truth to hive in it and make their sweet honey.

Come into the world, again, wild bees, wild bees!"

William Butler Yeats

EPILOGUE

REMEMBERING

DERMOT HEALY

Poet, Novelist, Dramatist, Mentor and Friend

THE SPIRIT WELL
OF WRITER DERMOT HEALY

*This piece was originally printed in
the Irish American cultural magazine **éirways** in 2015*

\

Ellen's Pub
Ballyconnell, Sligo – Ireland

It is 1998. Poor St. Anthony is covered in soot. So is poor Jesus. The saint's plaster is so black with decades of smoke and dust that you barely see him hidden high in the shadows. The Savior is easier to spot because his deep eyes look out lovingly and directly at your eye level. But the eyes must look through layers of soot covering his glass frame. And what was once a graphic flaming, blood-red, pierced heart glowing out of his bosom as if the chest were cut open, is now muddied to a brown of ethereal cow dung.

These tarnishings of saint and Savior are not the product of decades of smoky veneration from candles or incense of the sanctuary. They're the night-in, night-out dirty work of the smoke of cigarettes and turf fire.

Their venue is Ellen's Pub. It's hidden in a back road in this largely overlooked peninsula reaching out to the Atlantic. You might say it's a last pub in Ireland before Boston. For many a year from their place on the shelf and the wall of Ellen's, St. Anthony and the Savior have witnessed drink taken—copiously and often illegally late into the early hours. They have also been silent party to many a night when the "craic"—that high buzz of an evening of pints, banter and song—"was grand." Despite their soot stains, you get the feeling these two icons like it here. It's a helluva lot more fun than being stuck over some candles in a chilly church. And surely, from their listening post on the wall at Ellen's, these icons are privy to more of the human heart than any priest in the dark of the confessional.

It's early evening at Ellen's. This is the time when the poets like to converge after a day of fishing the seas of imagination. Later will come the farmers and the other kind of fishermen. The dusk of October is dropping earlier each evening now. Depending on the weather, a glimmer of setting sun or the bleak glow of overcast seeps through the small windows at the end of the bar.

Most evenings Dermot Healy comes in at this time. He chooses always the same stool—unofficially reserved for him like a pew in a church. It's his choice because it has a clear view of the window. Thus, he can as he chats hold in the corner of his eye the last of the light until it fades into black. In this part of the world, the approaching loss of summer light into winter dark is widely bemoaned as "seriously depressing." Another who watches the light dim into winter is Leland Bardwell, prolific poet and playwright. She speaks fast, in snippets whose wit you catch a few moments after they land, delivered in elegant, dramatic Anglo-Irish tone. She rolls her own cigarettes.

Ellen's Pub is not fancy. It is small and dirty. The ceiling is low. You find here none of the pretensions of the smart new pubs of Ireland that mimic the old ways with the likes of red-velour padded nooks and other inept renditions of idealized pubs of the past. Here at Ellen's the soiled, padded seat of every last bar stool is cracked. The glow of a lone fluorescent light sneaks from under a crooked shelf behind the bar. The rest is shadows. Michael, the owner and bartender—the publican—waits quietly for orders. He is dark eyed, soft spoken, and moves with the practiced smoothness of an undertaker.

Despite the shabby and shadowy ambience, Ellen's is in these parts a beacon of inner light of the kind an Irish spirit likes—the glow that comes from a mix of equal parts stout and talk under low ceilings. Because of this, Ellen's sooner or later in any week draws a visit from almost all the seeker souls drawn to this bare, spirit-windy landscape at the edge of the sea.

~~~

SO IT WAS, late one October afternoon in 1998 when, after settling in at a rented cottage down the road, I entered Ellen's for the first time. You might have called me just another seeker soul coming in the door. There was but one man at the bar. I thought he might be a fisherman. After a long shared silence, he spoke.

"Are you new round here?" I told him yes, I'd come to do some writing. "Do you have one of them computers?" he asked. Eventually, American style, I asked what kind of work he did. "I do a bit of writing myself," he answered. It was then he told me his name: Dermot Healy. By premonition of coincidence, a dear friend back in the States, just before I left for Ireland, had given me a gift of *The Bend for Home*, Healy's then best-selling memoir. That was the first I had heard of a Dermot Healy.

Our conversation was ignited. More coincidences. He was brought up in the town of Cavan, down the street from where my fabled, business-savvy spinster aunt, Baby Whelan, ran a fancy goods and confectionary shop. "You're not Baby Whelan's nephew!" he said amazed. As we spoke, there was a light like a votive candle in his eye. And a resonance of theater in his voice. And—I would come later to know—a wildness in his mind that was more than match for the patch of the end of earth that is Ballyconnell, Sligo.

The next night I came to dinner for the first time in the surreally sited home he had built with Helen, his wife, on the back side of a cliff at the edge of the sea, a spot where light seemed to play new games hour by hour. I learned later that year after year Healy would, like Sisyphus, work stubbornly, undauntedly, against the battering sea below, which was pulling back into its deep the giant rocks along the sands below his cliff.

A quirky friendship, in which he also took on a role of mentor, opened between us. Over fifteen years, on both sides of the Atlantic, it grew. For me, there was always a touch of enigma in it, but then again, many would say Dermot would be the definition of enigma. The friendship ended in sorrow on a night in June 2014. It was then, with no warning, death took Dermot—in his home above the sea and the rocks, up the road from Ellen's.

Michael Whelan